THE PRACTICE OF JOY WORKBOOK

Pamela Larde, PhD

Tandem Light Press
Atlanta, GA

The Practice of Joy Workbook:
Creating Revolutionary Change in our Personal and Professional Lives

Copyright © 2024 by Pamela A. Larde. All rights reserved.

Printed in the United States of America. No part of this book may be reproduced, scanned, or transmitted in any printed, electronic, mechanical, including photocopying, recording, or any information storage and retrieval system, without permission in writing from the publisher except in the case of reprints in the context of reviews. Please do not participate in or encourage piracy of copyrighted materials in violation of the author's rights.

Tandem Light Press paperback 2024
ISBN: 979-8-9882517-5-0

Contents

Gratitude from the Author — 2
Purpose of this Course — 3

Part I: Understanding Joy — **5**
Defining Joy — 6
The EPIC Joy Approach — 12

Part II: Creating Joy — **19**
Establish Well-Being — 20
Position People — 26
Integrate Joy Practices — 32
Create Revolutionary Change — 38

Part III: Practicing Joy — **49**
Barriers to Creating Joy — 50
Strategies for Creating Joy — 56

Reflection & Conclusion — 69
About the Author — 79

Gratitude from the Author

To My Fellow Joy Whisperers,

Your unwavering encouragement and support have been the driving force behind my journey of studying the practice and science of joy. Your belief in this work invigorates me to continue seeking out greater understanding of joy and of ways to curate joy in our lives.

Your kindness and dedication fuel my passion to show the world the true power of joy and strength. From the bottom of my heart, thank you for being a pillar of support. Your contribution, whether big or small, has made a significant difference in my mission. Let's continue this journey together, bringing joy and resilience to the forefront for those who need it most.

With sincere gratitude,

Dr. Pamela Larde
THE PRACTICE & SCIENCE OF JOY

Purpose of this Course

The Practice of Joy course is an ICF approved CCE course designed to be a transformative journey that can help participants unlock the true essence of peace and purpose within themselves as a means for executing greater levels of joy in their lives. This course offers an invaluable deep dive into our well-being and the curation of a life of joy that flows seamlessly through our personal and professional lives.

This course offers evidence-based techniques, including positive psychology concepts, reflection, and self-awareness exercises designed to offer practical approaches to cultivating joy through the highs and lows of life. We begin in Part One by getting clear on what joy is and how we might define it for ourselves. In Part Two, we explore the concept of joy more deeply with a strong emphasis on wellness; and in Part Three, we learn about the barriers to joy and how to employ strategies that enable us to overcome these barriers.

Through interactive lessons and practical exercises, this course demonstrates the power of finding keys to joy in meaningful connections while navigating challenges with mental stamina and resilience. *The Practice of Joy* is suitable for individuals representing a wide range of life experiences, seasons, and circumstances. Whether you are seeking a more joyful outlook on life, wishing to enhance your relationships, or yearning for a more fulfilling career, this course offers the opportrunity to gain the tools necessary to create joy through all of the highs and lows of life.

As you join this vibrant community of joy-seekers, you'll find that this this course offers an inspiring journey towards a life that many struggle to believe is possible. It begins with what you dare to envision. The ultimate goal is to challenge you to create a brighter and more hopeful future in every aspect of your life.

Getting Started

Before you get started, take the Journey of You Assessment as a starting point to this journey. This assessment contains 9 areas that represent a holistic look at the multi-faced nature of your life. This exercise assesses your level of satisfaction and range of expression in these areas as a snapshot in time. As you work through the questions, you may notice areas of strength and security and areas where you may want to improve your level of satisfaction and joy.

Scan the QR code below to access the assessment:

*"Joy does not simply happen to us.
We have to choose joy,
and keep choosing it every day."*

-Henri J.M. Nouwen

Part I
Understanding Joy

Defining Joy

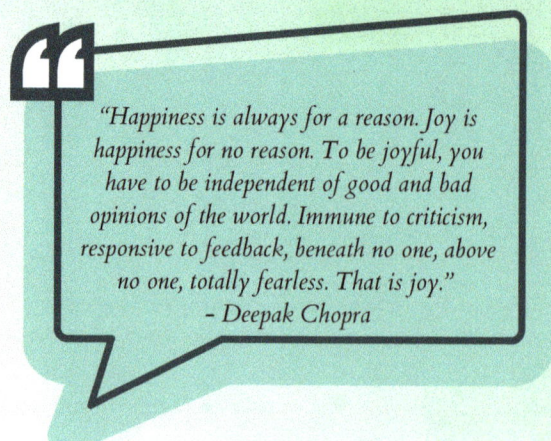

The American Psychological Association (APA) defines joy as: *"A feeling of extreme gladness, delight, or exhilaration of the spirit arising from a sense of well-being or satisfaction."*

Notice that this definition describes joy as something that arises from a sense of well-being rather than from the occurrence of a specific event. Across disciplines, beliefs, and philosophies, this idea of joy transcending what is happening seems to be the greatest commonality of how we understand joy. In this course, we expand this definition of joy to include:

"An intentional approach to life that centers well-being through both positive and negative experiences."

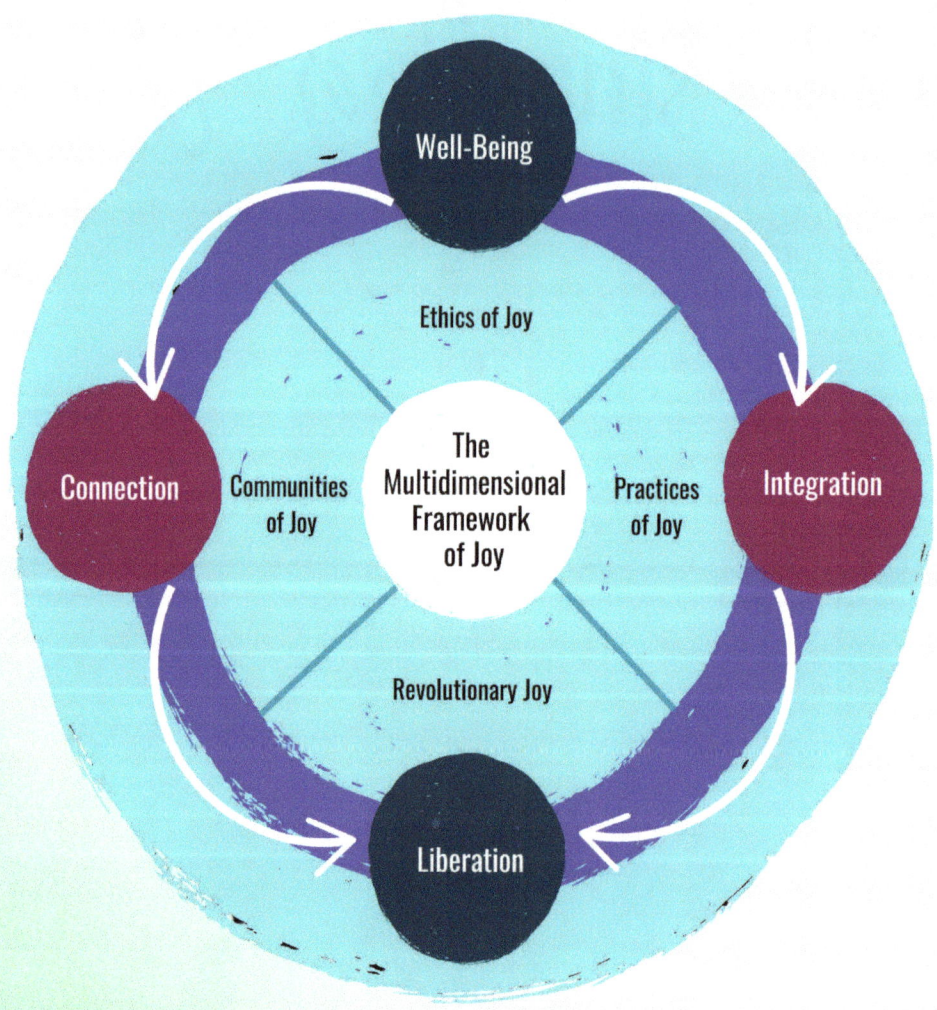

Defining Joy

The Multidimensional Framework of Joy presents an interconnected approach to describing how joy is rooted, nurtured, and manifested to create radical change. This framework consists of four key dimensions that contribute to our joy: well-being, connection, integration, and liberation. Well-being is the root of joy, connection and integration are nurturers of joy, and liberation is the manifestation of joy. As other researchers have found, and as stated in the American Psychological Association's definition, joy is rooted in a place of well-being.

The condition of our well-being, whether in a high or low state, informs the connections we experience with other people and the ways in which we integrate our joy. The strength of our communities and our practices have a liberating power that brings freedom from oppression, limiting beliefs, varying forms of trauma. Liberation is where we face our difficult truths, discover our whole selves, and create the change that we yearn to see. This interdisciplinary framework is grounded in scientific work around trauma, well-being, self-determination, shadow work, human connection, and belonging.

pause & reflect

What does joy mean to you? Write down your thoughts.

_____
_____
_____
_____
_____
_____
_____
_____
_____
_____

Defining Joy

The Difference Between Happiness and Joy

Happiness requires an environment that yields positive feelings in response to what is happening in that environment. It is what we feel when we experience positive events. It is our natural reaction to stimuli that gives us pleasure. The pleasure that leads to our feelings of happiness can be healthy, but it can also be toxic. Thus, the risk of solely relying on happiness is that it is about feeling good regardless of whether or not we are *living well*. This can lead to addictive, self-soothing behaviors that fail to create long-term peace of mind, as happiness can be fleeting. The benefits of happiness, however, can be immense when used strategically, as it can relieve stress, raise motivation, and improve our mood.

While happiness can enhance well-being, joy is *rooted* in our well-being. It exists in both enjoyable and challenging environments. Joy is more than a feeling. It is a values-driven practice that we take on as a lifestyle and resilience strategy. It endures despite the environment that surrounds us. This means that we can create and experience joy even when we are having difficult times. The concepts of happiness and joy both have profound value and certainly intersect in some ways, but they also have notable differences that are important to understand as we explore what it means to live a life of joy.

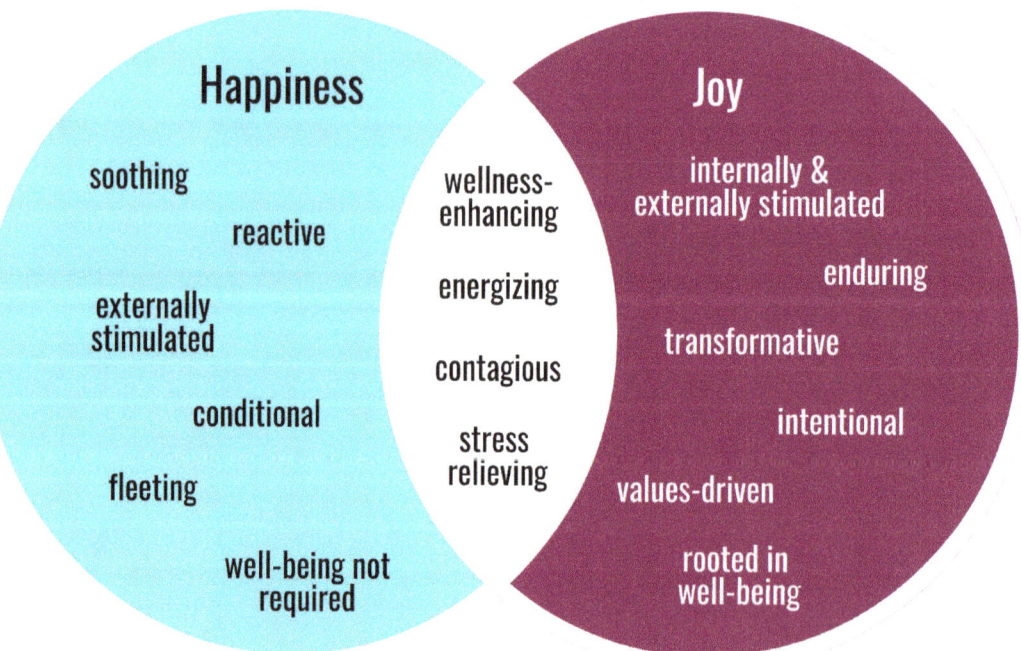

Defining Joy

We can draw upon our joy with intention, particularly when needed during difficult times. In this sense, it is transformative. Joy works from the inside out, and from the outside in to strengthen our will to persist through struggle and endures as long as we nurture our well-being.

pause & reflect

What specific activities or hobbies consistently bring a sense of joy and fulfillment into your life?

Defining Joy

pause & reflect

How do you describe the difference between happiness and joy? Write your thoughts in the space below and then use the graphic to fill in your own words, experiences, and values.

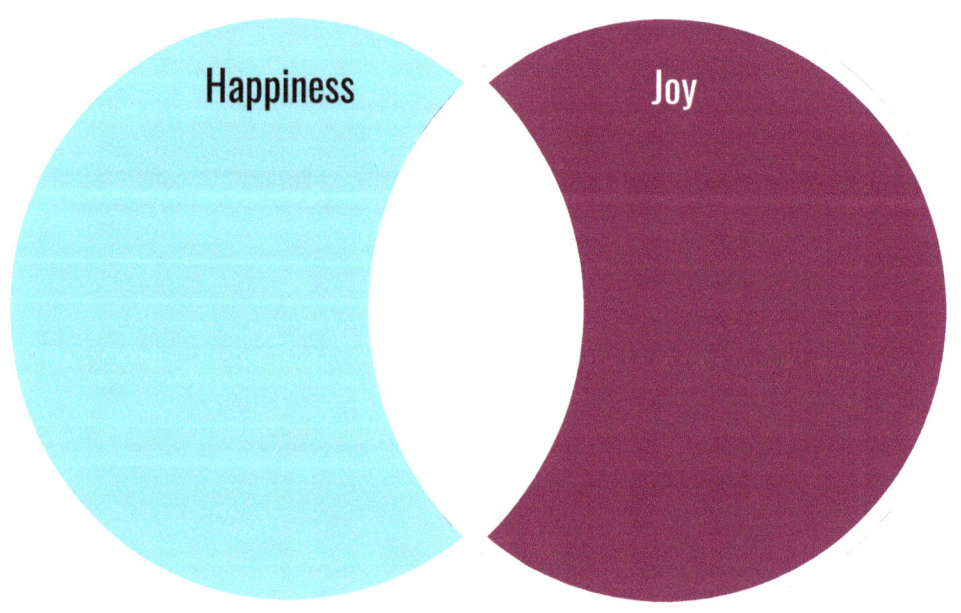

pause & reflect

Scan the QR Code below to listen to a childhood story about the difference between happiness and joy. What does your own childhood story reveal about your journey to joy?

Defining Joy

The EPIC Joy Approach

Step 1:
E is for Eudaimonia
(Establish Well-Being)

Step 2:
P is for People
(Position People)

Step 3:
I is for Integration
(Integrate Joy Practices)

Step 4:
C is for Change
(Create Revolutionary Change)

The EPIC Joy Approach

The EPIC Joy approach is an actionable, practical model derived from and rooted in the more conceptual Multidimensional Framework of Joy. This framework consists of four key dimensions—Well-Being, Connection, Integration, and Liberation—that provide a foundation for understanding how joy can be cultivated and sustained in our lives. The EPIC Joy approach translates these dimensions into practical steps that empower individuals to experience joy in a tangible and transformative way.

Eudaimonia (Establish Well-Being)
Eudaimonia is the Greek concept of flourishing, embodying a state of being that goes beyond momentarily feeling good and emphasizes the value of being well. It involves cultivating a life aligned with purpose, fulfillment, and deep personal values. In the EPIC Joy approach, establishing well-being means actively nurturing your physical, emotional, and mental health, so you have a strong foundation for joy to thrive. It is centered around finding harmony between all aspects of being and flourishing as your most authentic self.

People (Position People)
Joy is often found in connection. The "People" component is about recognizing the power of our relationships and choosing how to position people in our lives. Not everyone adds to our joy, and some connections can even diminish it. As we intentionally determine who to keep close and who to establish boundaries with, we create meaningful relationships that support and amplify our joy. The goal is to curate a circle of support that helps us grow.

Integration (Integrate Joy)
Integration is the practice of weaving joy into every aspect of our daily lives. It involves the intentional habits and rituals that allow joy to become a natural and consistent part of how we live, work, and relate to others. Integrating joy—from small moments like savoring a cup of tea to larger practices like celebrating milestones—helps us create a life where joy is not an afterthought, but a guiding principle. This component empowers us to normalize joy as essential rather than a luxury.

Change (Create Revolutionary Change)
Joy can be a catalyst for transformation. The "change" component emphasizes the importance of harnessing joy to initiate shifts in our lives. This can mean creating a plot twist in your career, redefining your relationships, or starting a new project. Joy is an empowering force that helps us manifest and sustain change. Creating change enables us to move toward what serves our well-being and letting go of what doesn't. This means engaging in acts that liberate us from barriers and lead to more fulfilling lives.

The EPIC Joy Approach

pause & reflect

What moments or experiences in your personal life bring you the most joy? How do these moments affect your overall well-being?

_____
_____
_____
_____
_____
_____
_____
_____
_____

In your professional life, can you identify instances where you have experienced genuine joy? What factors contributed to these moments?

_____
_____
_____
_____
_____
_____
_____
_____

What recurring patterns or situations tend to drain your joy in your personal life? How do you cope with these situations?

_____
_____
_____
_____
_____
_____
_____
_____

What challenges or obstacles have you encountered in your professional life that have led to a diminished sense of joy? How do you cope with these challenges?

_____
_____
_____
_____
_____
_____
_____
_____

The EPIC Joy Approach

What factors do you believe contribute to the presence of joy in your life?

_____
_____
_____
_____
_____
_____

What mindsets or beliefs might be influencing your experience of joy? How might these affect both personal and professional aspects of your life?

_____
_____
_____
_____
_____
_____

What external influences, such as relationships, environments, or societal expectations impact your ability to experience joy?

_____
_____
_____
_____
_____
_____

What commonalities exist between the situations or contexts where you feel the most joyful? What can you learn from these patterns?

_____
_____
_____
_____
_____
_____
_____
_____
_____
_____

On the flip side, what <u>recurring</u> situations hinder your ability to experience joy? How can you address or navigate these situations differently?

_____
_____
_____
_____
_____
_____
_____
_____
_____
_____

Notes

Part II
Creating Joy

Establish Well-Being

Step 1:
 is for Eudaimonia
(Establish Well-Being)

Establish Well-Being

STEP 1: ESTABLISH WELL-BEING

Eudaimonia involves embodying a state of being that goes beyond momentarily feeling good and emphasizes the value of being well. Well-being is the extent to which we are able to experience greater levels of flourishing and reduced levels of languishing. When we flourish, we are in a state of positive well-being and experience feelings of happiness, fulfillment, and purpose in life. It means we have high levels of well-being, positive emotions, and social functioning, and are able to cope effectively with challenges and stressors. Languishing, on the other hand, is a state of low well-being in which we experience feelings of emptiness, apathy, and disconnection from others. When we languish, we have low levels of well-being, negative emotions, ineffective social functioning, and struggle to cope with stress and challenges.

The Ethics of Joy

The ethics of joy is the extent to which our joy flows from and is expressed by the state of our well-being. If we are well, our joy may be progressive and reflects that wellness. If we are struggling with well-being, and that struggle remains unaddressed, the way we exude our joy may be regressive and reflective of our lack of well-being. We are generally not all one or the other, nor do all areas of our lives demonstrate joy in the same way. Depending on the state of our well-being in a particular area of life, we may find ourselves at different points on that continuum. The ethics arise in our subsequent behaviors, determining the extent to which we value the well-being of ourselves and others through the pursuit and maintenance of our joy.

Let's illustrate this as an analogy of drawing from two different wells of water. The first is the languishing well, which represents a low state of well-being and a mindset that leads to regressive joy. The second is the flourishing well, which represents a high state of well-being and a mindset that leads to progressive joy.

The Flourishing Well

Progressive Joy

Authentic (toward self)
Vicarious (toward others)

The Languishing Well

Regressive Joy

Toxic (toward self)
Malicious (toward others)

Establish Well-Being

The Flourishing Well: The flourishing well nurtures our health and well-being. It represents freedom and fulfillment and involves savoring our lives, maintaining life-giving relationships with others, finding fulfillment in purpose, and experiencing peace. When we draw from the flourishing well and strive toward a higher state of well-being, the joy we embody can be progressive and can facilitate our growth. It is how we celebrate what we love about life and how we find our strength when the journey becomes difficult.

- Authentic progressive joy: rooted in well-being and thrives as we pursue wellness, but can also be externally driven, as we can ignite it when we *need* to feel well.

- Vicarious progressive joy: the joy we feel for other people when they experience joy. It is an invigoration of the spirit driven by the positive experiences of others and is rooted in our already-existing internal wellspring of joy.

The Languishing Well: The languishing well is counterproductive to our health and well-being and represents deep pain. It involves the struggle to find enjoyment in life and is reminiscent of a loss of control, a fear of losing something of value, or the impact of unresolved trauma. When we draw our nourishment from the languishing well, the perceived joy we embody can actually be regressive or diminishing to ourselves and others.

- Toxic regressive joy: finding satisfaction, relief, and pleasure in behaviors that feel good, but ultimately cause us personal harm—like excessive drug use, reckless driving, or binge eating.

- Malicious regressive joy: finding satisfaction in behaviors and outcomes that specifically cause harm to others—like seeking revenge or diminishing someone's sense of worth.

Establish Well-Being

pause & reflect

Regressive joy might manifest in toxic behaviors or malicious intentions towards oneself or others. Reflect on an experience in which you found your joy in a negative, regressive way. How would you describe your state of well-being and your relationships with others during this time?

Well-Being

Relationships

Establish Well-Being

Which of the two wells (languishing or flourishing) do you feel most connected to in your current state of well-being?

_____
_____
_____
_____
_____
_____
_____
_____

How is your current state of well-being impacting the way you experience joy?

_____
_____
_____
_____
_____
_____
_____
_____
_____
_____

Establish Well-Being

Reflect on a moment when you experienced joy in a positive and progressive way. What words come to mind when you think of that experience?

How does vicarious joy influence your relationships and your sense of connection with others?

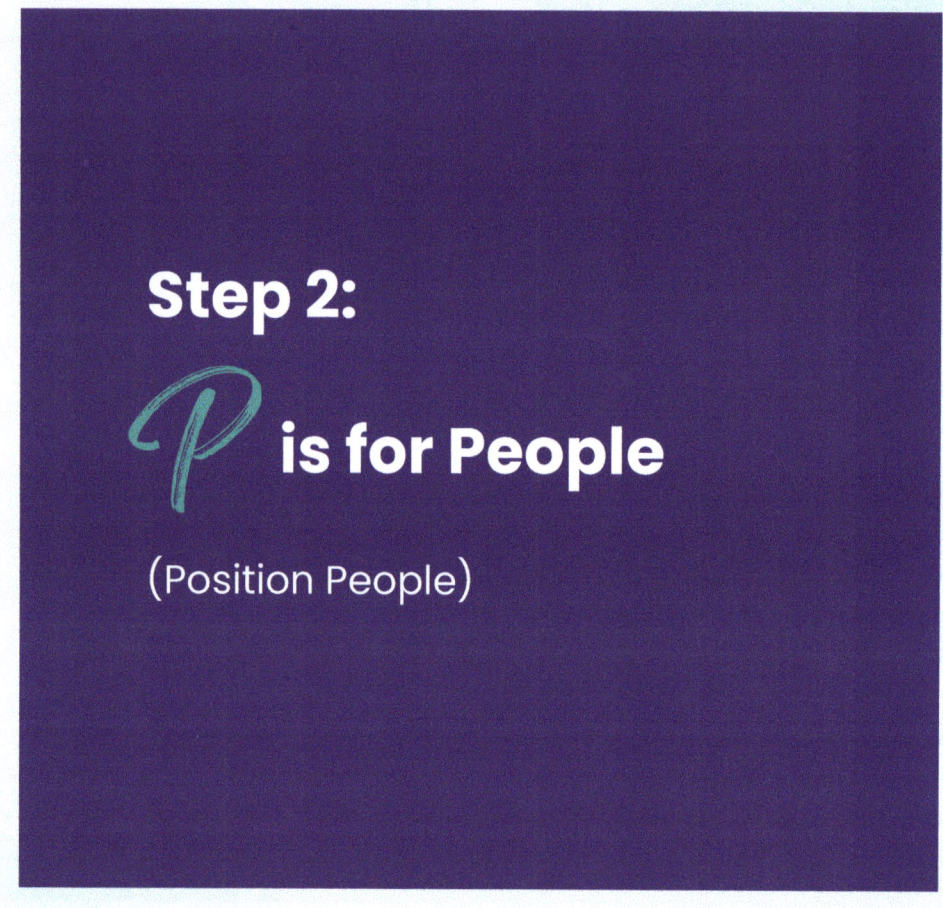

STEP 2: POSITION PEOPLE

The Communities of Joy Model

The Communities of Joy Model includes three layers of connection that enable us to assess the value people bring to our lives and how to position them accordingly. The layers include our core community, our circle community, and our fragmented community. All are present in our lives and all can have a profound impact on our joy. Understanding who these connections are—and the role they play in our lives—is key to our ability to maintain progressive joy and to create change in ourselves and others.

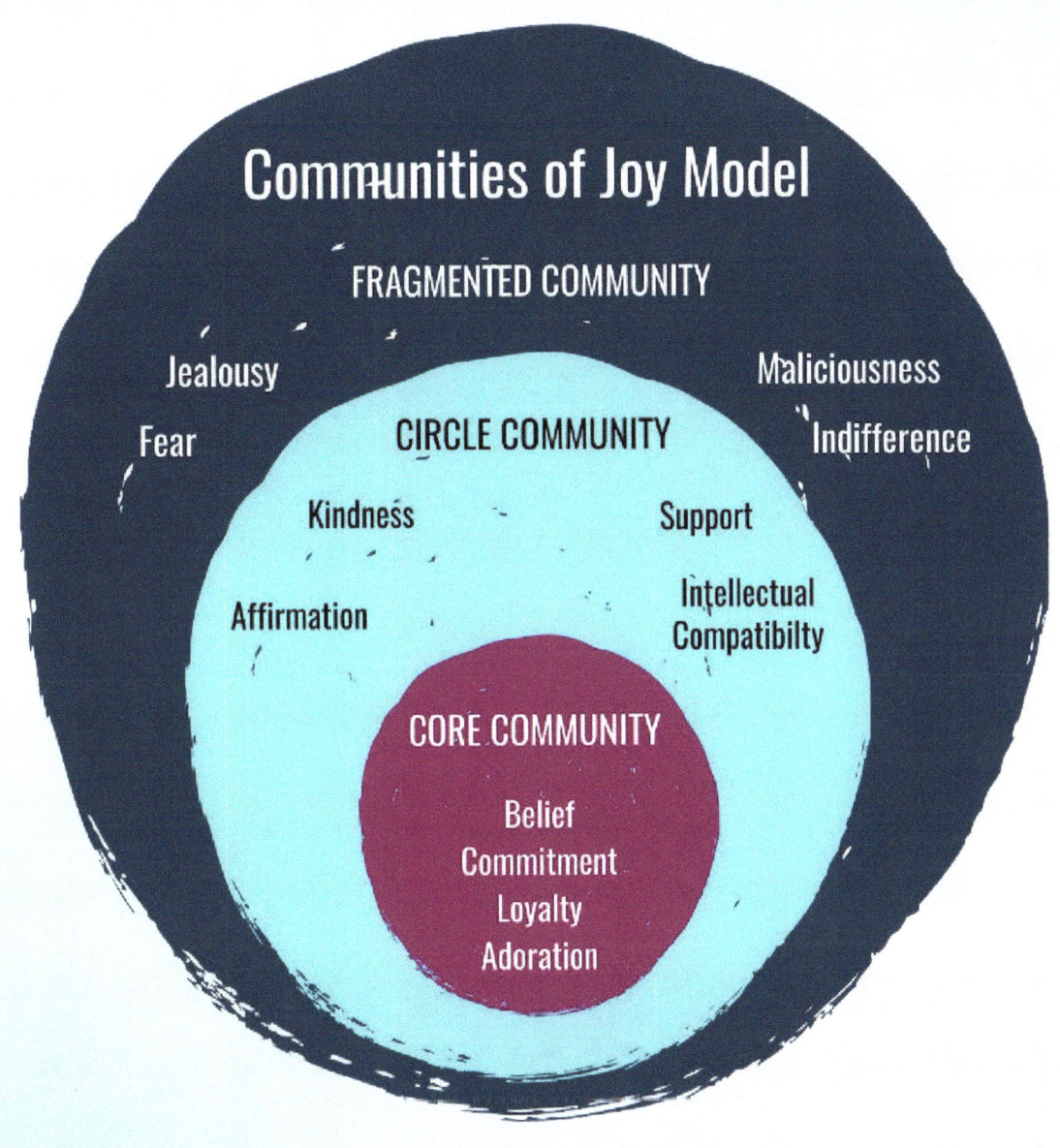

Position People

Fragmented Community

Those who pose threats to our joy. They are <u>fearful</u>, <u>malicious</u>, <u>indifferent</u>, or <u>jealous</u>. Only one of these characteristics is needed for a person to be a part of our fragmented community.

Core Community

Those who reflect all four of the circle characteristics, but also have four even deeper characteristics: <u>belief</u>, <u>commitment</u>, <u>loyalty</u>, and <u>adoration</u>. They are the people we can trust with our vulnerability.

Circle Community

Key to our growth and development. Our circle community can be recognizable by four key characteristics: they are <u>kind</u> to us, they are <u>supportive</u>, they <u>affirm</u> our strengths, or they are <u>intellectually compatible</u>.

Use the dotted gridlines below to create a visual representation of the connections in your life.

Positioning People with the Communities of Joy Model

The connections we create with other people and the networks we are a part of have the power to either nurture or stifle our joy. When we experience high levels of well-being, the people that surround us add to that well-being and are more likely to nurture and facilitate joy in our lives. When we experience prolonged low levels of well-being reminiscent of languishing, we are more likely to gravitate to connections that diminish and block our joy, or nurture a joy that brings harm to others. With self-awareness, we can be more conscious of the connections we choose and avoid attaching ourselves to trauma bonds, co-dependent relationships, and connections that temporarily soothe our pain.

Use the space below to write in names of people who fit into each your communities of joy.

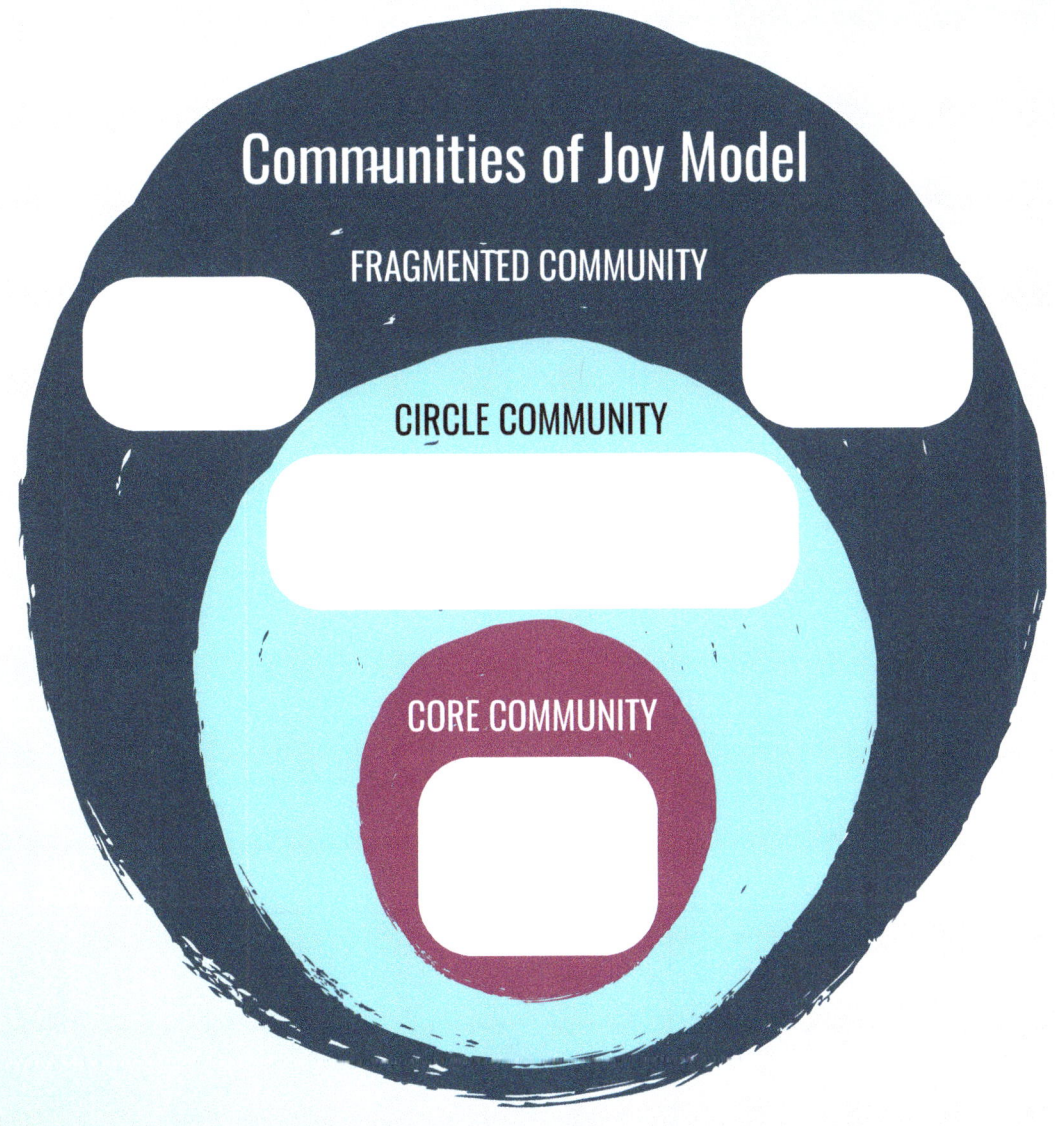

Position People

pause & reflect

Reflect on the individuals in your life who pose threats to your joy. How can you strategize to protect your joy from these threats?

_____
_____
_____
_____
_____
_____
_____

Consider the key circle connections in your life? How do they contribute to your growth and well-being?

_____
_____
_____
_____
_____
_____
_____
_____
_____

Position People

Position People

How can you nurture relationships with your circle connections to enhance your joy?

_____
_____
_____
_____
_____
_____
_____
_____

Consider the members of your core community. Describe the importance of trust and adoration in these core connections and how they impact your joy.

_____
_____
_____
_____
_____
_____
_____
_____
_____
_____

DIMENSION 3: INTEGRATE JOY PRACTICES

Integration, also dependent on well-being, addresses how we live out four distinct practices of joy. Understanding the practice of joy and how to integrate these practices into our lives enables us to utilize our joy with intention. The four practices include: the **ethos** we embody, the **experiences** we create, the **emotions** we exude, and the **expressions** we share.

Integrate Joy Practices

pause & reflect

How have you integrated joy in your life through your ethos, experiences, emotions, and expressions? Use the graphic below to map out your practices in each category.

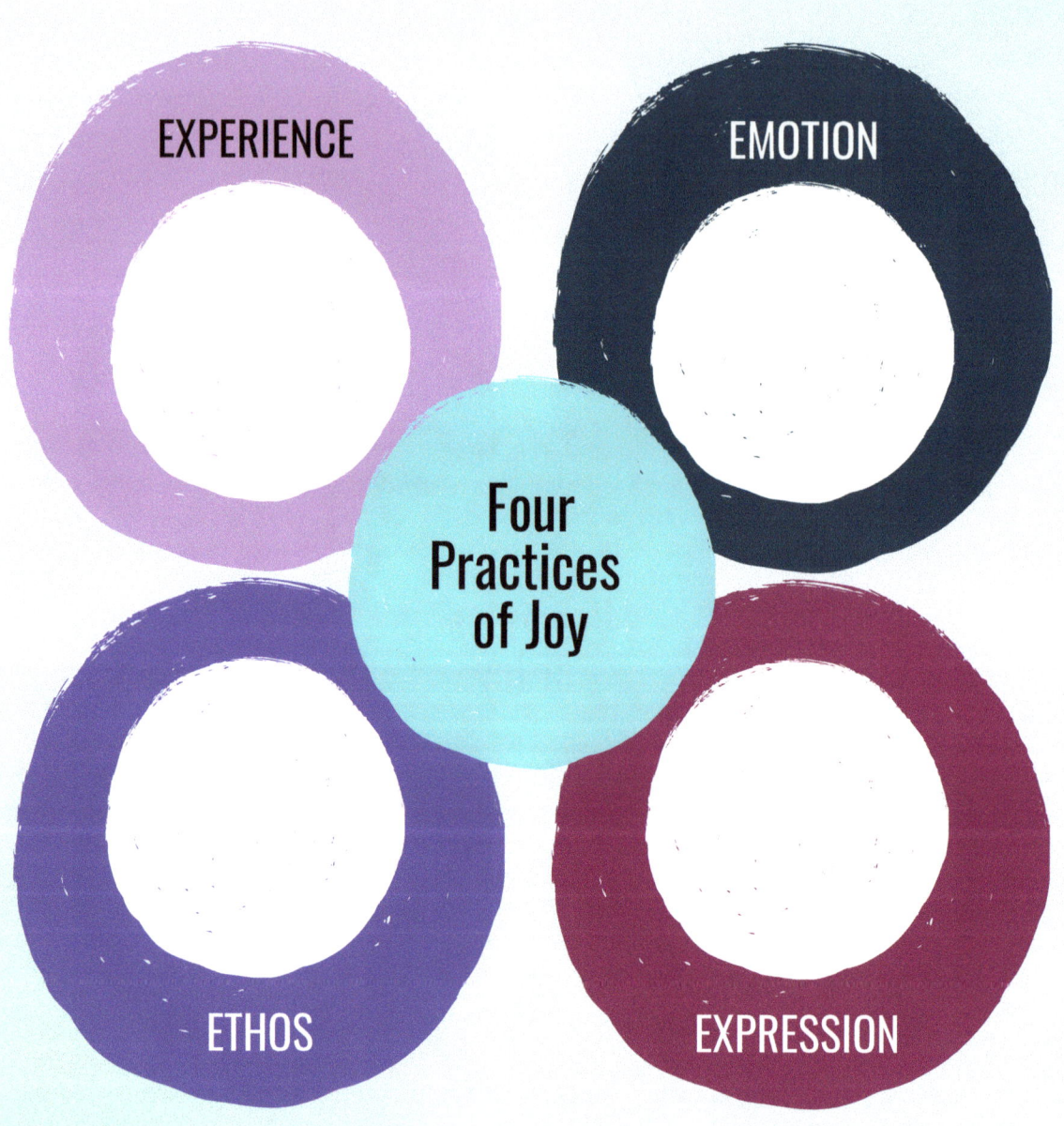

Integrate Joy Practices

How closely does your current personal and professional life align with your values and passions? In what ways might aligning more closely bring about greater joy?

_____
_____
_____
_____
_____
_____
_____
_____

What aspects of your personal and professional life need to be reevaluated or adjusted to better align with your sense of joy?

_____
_____
_____
_____
_____
_____
_____
_____
_____

Integrate Joy Practices

What specific changes or adjustments you can make to your daily routines, habits, or interactions to create a more joyful environment?

___

In your professional life, how can you actively seek out opportunities or moments that align with your personal definition of joy?

___

Notes

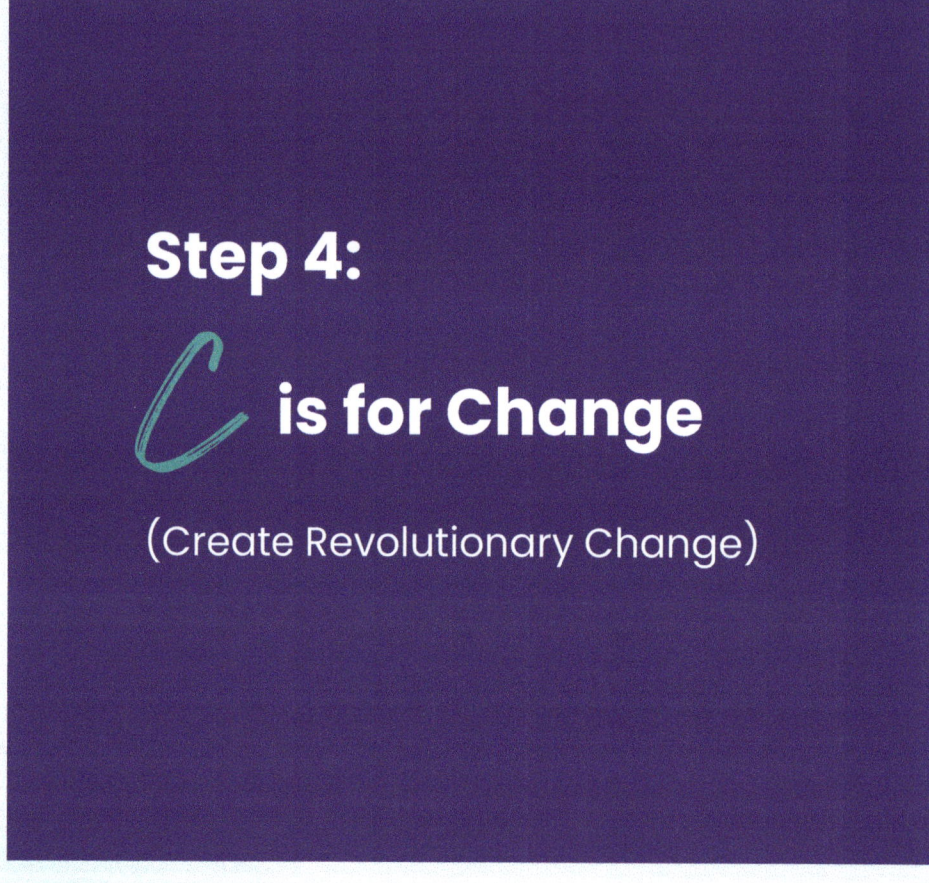

DIMENSION 4: CREATE REVOLUTIONARY CHANGE

Change and liberation represents personal and social freedom from interpersonal barriers, mindsets, and structures that stifle our joy. When we start a revolution, we do so because we've reached a breaking point and have decided that we will no longer tolerate the system and corresponding beliefs that govern our actions, perspectives of self, and social norms.

Visually, this model is reminiscent of a triad symbol, which represents the never-ending motion and cycle of life. So long as we are alive, we are ever-growing and evolving. Regardless of where we are in our life journey, this model offers a roadmap for stepping into our own revolutions to create a life we can genuinely love.

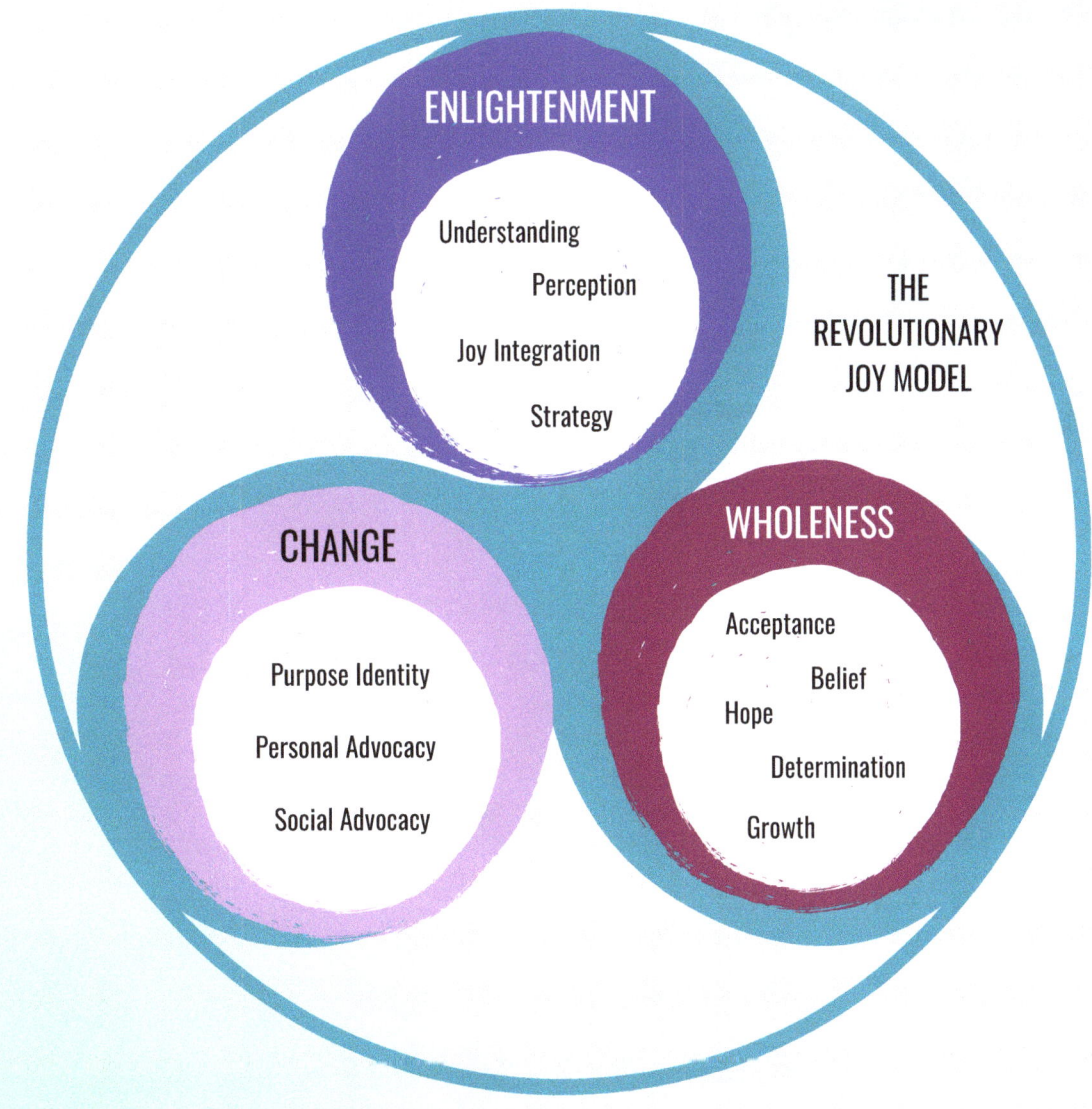

Create Revolutionary Change

Pursuing Enlightenment: Demonstrates how we educate ourselves about the life circumstances we are facing. When we can name this phase of our lives with confidence and when we come to realize our power, we better position ourselves to strategize around ways to make the most of this journey. This is a process of seeking understanding, checking perceptions, integrating joy, and engaging strategically.

Pursuing Wholeness: Is what it means to introduce yourself to you. Our whole selves consist of what is seen (uncovered and exposed to the light) and what is unseen (covered and protected in the shadows). This enables us to engage our whole selves and to experience the power of that wholeness through acceptance, belief, hope, determination, and growth.

Pursuing Change: Compels us to understand our purpose. As we heighten this understanding, we position ourselves to create change in three ways: by discovering our purpose identity, by advocating for ourselves, and by advocating for others.

pause & reflect

How do you envision revolutionary joy in your life? Draw a picture of what that might look like below:

Create Revolutionary Change

What steps can you take to gain a deeper understanding of your life circumstances and embrace the power to change?

_____
_____
_____
_____
_____
_____
_____
_____

What are some barriers or mindsets that currently stifle your joy?

Create Revolutionary Change

The Reverse Domino Effect

The Reverse Domino Effect involves five milestones that include acceptance, belief, hope, determination, and growth. These milestones facilitate reversing the effects of trauma and hardship as a strategy for creating growth and healing. As we move to create a reverse domino effect in our lives, we gradually release the shadows and uncover ourselves. We accept who we are; we surround ourselves with the people who accept us; we believe in ourselves; we have hope for our future and believe that what we need will be available to us when we need it; we are motivated to act by moving through fear; and we address the pain so it does not hinder us from walking and living in purpose. When we create a reverse domino effect, we reverse whatever has held us back and clear the way to step forward.

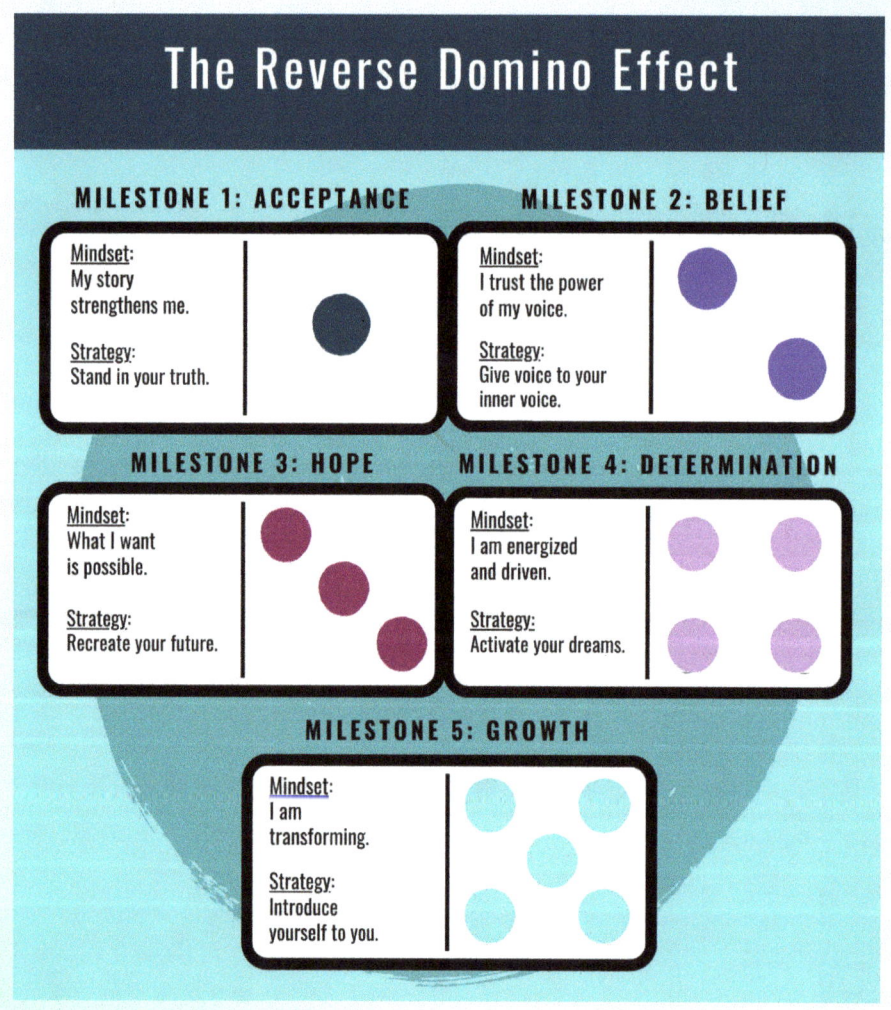

Create Your Own Reverse Domino Effect

What are three challenges in my life that hinder my joy?	In what areas of life do I struggle with acceptance? How do I wish for this to change?
In what areas of life do I struggle with belief? How do I wish for this to change?	In what areas of life do I struggle with hope? How do I wish for this to change?
In what areas of life do I struggle with determination? How do I wish for this to change?	In what areas of life do I struggle with growth? How do I wish for this to change?

Create Revolutionary Change

The Elements of Self-Love

The elements represent the four parts of a whole, indicating that self love takes on multiple roles that we may use all at once or primarily one at a time. This perspective of self-love allows us to give ourselves grace in terms of how we see ourselves and understand how we may care for ourselves differently depending on the circumstances we are facing at any given time. When we acknowledge these varied approaches to self-love, we enable ourselves to see unconventional approaches that are traditionally not seen as self-love. It is our self-love that advocates for what we need, so it may not look like going to day spas and getting massages. It may look like keeping an escape kit in the trunk of the car so that we can leave as soon as it is safe to do so.

Elements of Self-Love

Survivalist — the natural instinct to fight for our lives

Romantic — falling in love with our transformed or renewed selves

Superficial — practicing self-love when we don't yet feel it

Emancipatory — liberation from limiting behaviors, beliefs, or situations

pause & reflect

Use the graphic below to write in your answers to the following questions:

- In what areas of your life are you experiencing survivalist self-love?
- In what areas of your life are you experiencing romantic self-love?
- In what areas of your life you experiencing superficial self-love?
- In what areas of your life are you experiencing emancipatory self-love?

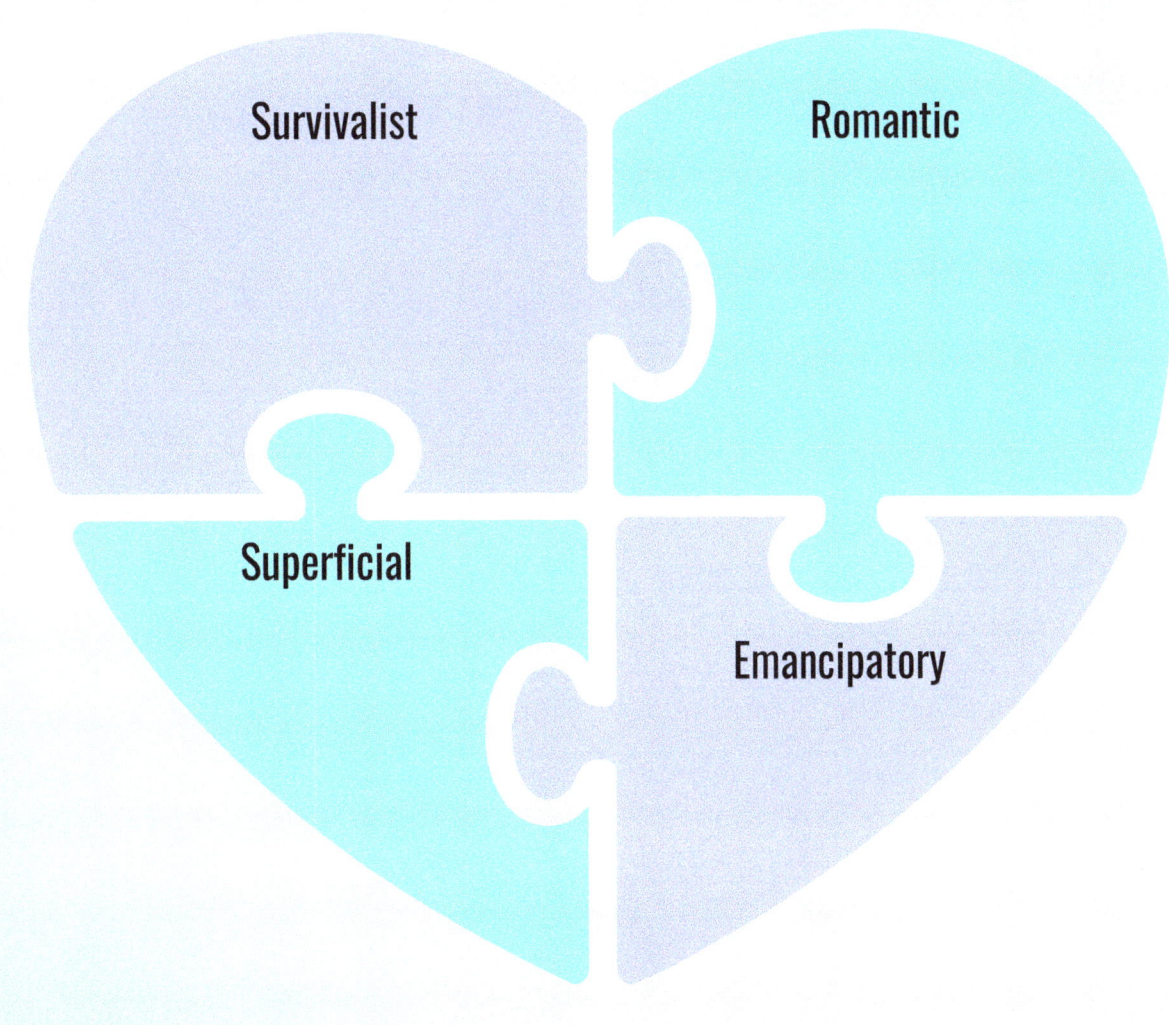

Create Revolutionary Change

Based on your answers on the previous page, reflect on the following and write your answers into the boxes below:

- What is working well in your self-love journey?
- What would you like to change about your self-love journey?

Working Well

Needs to Change

Notes

*"Don't merely fake it until you make it.
Practice it until you become it."*

-Dr. Pamela A. Larde

Part III
Practicing Joy

Barriers to Practicing Joy

OVERCOMING BARRIERS TO JOY

When it comes to cultivating joy, the intention part is important because there are always opposing forces that compel us to lean more into our pain than into joy. We are familiar with our pain. It doesn't let us down. It is predictable and relatable. Standing against the familiarity with pain that compels us to resist joy requires that we know that this resistance exists and that we have a strategy for overcoming it. The sections to follow describe six common barriers to joy that stem from our mindsets and beliefs, as well as the mindsets and beliefs of other people. These barriers include *negativity bias and habituation, fear of failure, moving in silence, imposter accusations, guilting,* and *shaming*. When we internalize these mindsets and beliefs, we are likely to "tone down" the joy to alleviate our own internal struggles and the struggles others project onto us. Everyone loses when this happens because we are not living our full joyful selves and others are deprived of the light we have the potential to shine.

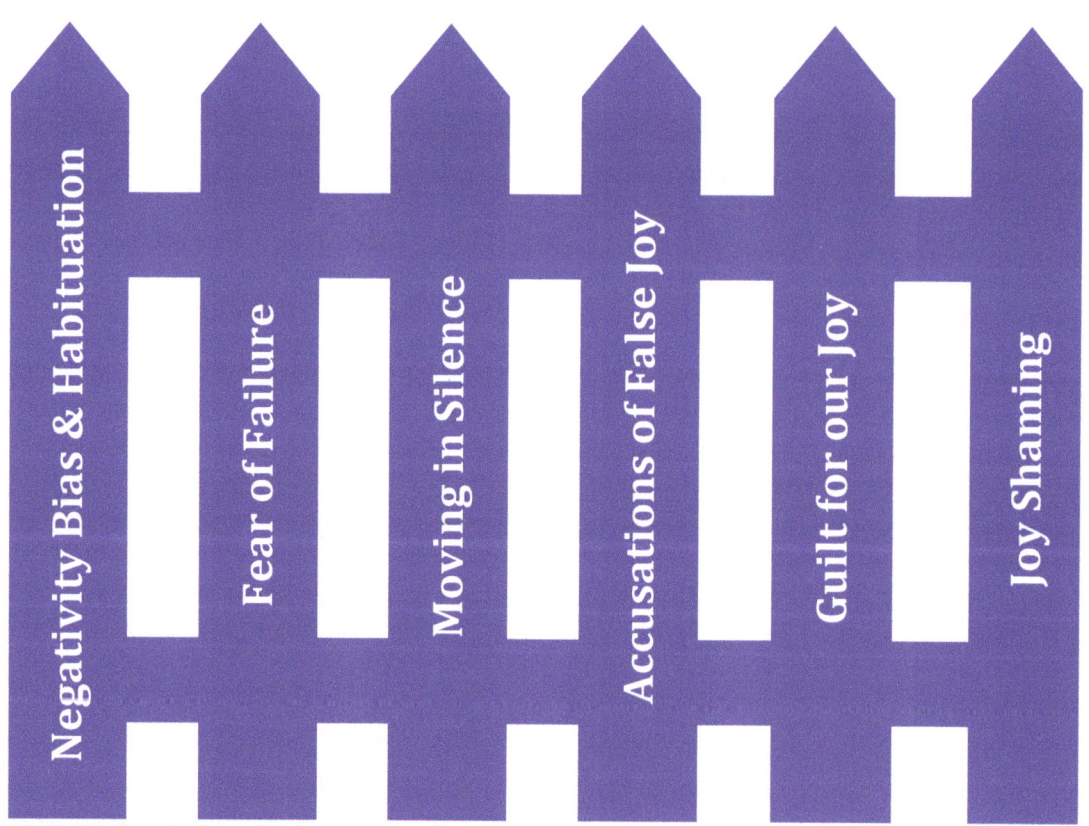

Barriers to Practicing Joy

Negativity Bias & Habituation

Negativity bias is our tendency to focus heavily on negative possibilities. **Habituation** is when we numb ourselves to the positive moments we experience on a day-to-day basis. Together, the two block our ability to experience joy.

Fear of Failure

This is a debilitating self-perception that compels us to base our decisions on an unjustified assumption of the worst case scenario, also referred to as *the low dream*. In such cases, we may opt to play it safe rather than step out on a limb to reach for something that our hearts desire.

Moving in Silence

Moving in silence essentially requires that we stifle our emotions and stuff them deep inside so that no one can threaten to steal our joy. This is, in fact, a well-known barrier to joy as expressing our joy yields more experiences of joy.

Accusations of False Joy

This is a limiting belief that counters the experience of joy resilience. It is grounded in the idea that finding joy through hardship is a myth and false positive behavior. These accusations are projected onto those who work to create joy through moments of struggle.

Guilt for our Joy

This is the feeling of inadequacy or unworthiness we internalize for experiencing joy in the presence of others. This is especially apparent when faced with others who are experiencing hardship or are struggling to find joy. This guilt can be internally or externally driven.

Joy Shaming

This refers to the act of oppressing and criticizing others for their sources or expressions of joy. This could manifest as criticizing, mocking, or diminishing the joy of others with the intention to silence, stifle liberation, or dehumanize an individual or group of people.

Barriers to Practicing Joy

pause & reflect

Consider a moment when you resisted experiencing joy due to familiar feelings of pain or discomfort. What do you think contributed to your hesitation to step into the joy?

_____
_____
_____
_____
_____
_____
_____

How do you think your own mindset and beliefs influence your tendency to lean towards pain or resistance rather than embracing joy?

_____
_____
_____
_____
_____
_____
_____
_____

Barriers to Practicing Joy

Among the six barriers to joy (negativity bias and habituation, fear of failure, moving in silence, imposter accusations, guilting, and shaming), which do you resonate with most? What is one strategy you can practice to overcome these barriers?

_____
_____
_____
_____
_____
_____
_____
_____

How might these barriers manifest differently in your personal life compared to your professional life?

_____
_____
_____
_____
_____
_____
_____
_____
_____

Barriers to Practicing Joy

Reflect on a time when you toned down your joy due to internal struggles or external pressures. How did this impact your own sense of well-being and the way you interacted with others?

_____
_____
_____
_____
_____
_____
_____
_____

Can you recall any situations where you observed someone else suppressing their joy due to similar barriers? How did their actions affect the overall atmosphere or dynamics of the situation?

_____
_____
_____
_____
_____
_____
_____
_____
_____
_____

Barriers to Practicing Joy

What negative beliefs or thought patterns have you identified within yourself that contribute to these barriers? How do these beliefs influence your overall attitude towards joy?

_____
_____
_____
_____
_____
_____
_____
_____

How might acknowledging and challenging these negative beliefs help you create space for more joy in your life?

_____
_____
_____
_____
_____
_____
_____
_____

Strategies for Practicing Joy

JOY RESILIENCE

Joy resilience is a strategy for overcoming hardship or trauma. It is how we rebuild relationships, fight oppression and injustice, and how we grow after a personal battle with health, addiction, financial hardships, or heartbreak. Joy springs from our well-being, and joy resilience uses that well-being to overcome threats to our livelihood. Its power is in our mindset, which enables us to find peace in situations that challenge us the most. It is a stellar ability to recalibrate our perceptions in a way that enables us to keep pushing through when we face seemingly hopeless situations.

Mental Stamina

Getting through the toughest moments of our lives—when it is most difficult to experience joy—requires a level of mental stamina that does not always come naturally. This typically requires strategy and intention. There are five strategies that make mental stamina work: people, projects, prayer, practice, and patience. These strategies are tools that enable us to move through our challenges with vision and intention.

Strategies for Practicing Joy

ACTIVATING MENTAL STAMINA

CHALLENGE #1

Describe the challenge you'd like to address in the space below. Use the prompt on the right to identify your strategies for addressing the challenge.

Challenge:

STRATEGIES for Mental Stamina

PEOPLE

PROJECTS

PRAYER

PATIENCE

PRACTICE

Strategies for Practicing Joy

ACTIVATING MENTAL STAMINA

CHALLENGE #2

Describe the challenge you'd like to address in the space below. Use the prompt on the right to identify your strategies for addressing the challenge.

Challenge:

STRATEGIES for Mental Stamina

PEOPLE

PROJECTS

PRAYER

PATIENCE

PRACTICE

Strategies for Practicing Joy

ACTIVATING MENTAL STAMINA

CHALLENGE #3

Describe the challenge you'd like to address in the space below. Use the prompt on the right to identify your strategies for addressing the challenge.

Challenge:

STRATEGIES for Mental Stamina

PEOPLE

PROJECTS

PRAYER

PATIENCE

PRACTICE

Strategies for Practicing Joy

Strategically Overcoming Barriers

Awareness of Joy Gaps *Tracking Joy*	**Permission** to Embody Joy *Dismantling Limiting Beliefs*	**Access** to Agency *Identifying Zones of Agency*
• Understanding the baseline and expanding what's possible	• Moving beyond contentment • Overcoming guilt, fear of disappointment, and disbelief	• Defining career joy possibilities • Engaging in the pursuit of joy

SETTING THE STAGE TO PURSUE JOY

Overcoming barriers to joy involves setting the stage for joy by becoming aware of what limits our capacity for joy, giving ourselves permission to fully embody joy, and recognizing our own agency.

Awareness of Joy Gaps: Identifying the gaps in our current experience of joy requires us to honestly evaluate our lives and recognize where joy may be missing. This helps us establish a baseline of where we currently stand and create opportunities to expand what is possible. This awareness is crucial for understanding what holds us back, whether it is external circumstances, internal beliefs, or unexamined habits. When we know where the gaps are, we can take steps to address them and invite more joy into our lives.

Permission to Embody Joy: Giving ourselves permission to fully embody joy means dismantling the limiting beliefs that keep us from experiencing true fulfillment. Moving beyond contentment requires us to confront and overcome these feelings of guilt, fear, and disbelief. We must learn to view joy as our birthright and not as something that needs to be justified. This enables us to move past the mental blocks that prevent us from fully embracing joy.

Access to Agency: Recognizing our own agency is about understanding the power we have to shape our experiences and create joy in our lives. As we identify our zones of agency—areas where we have influence and control—we can define new possibilities for career and life joy. When we understand and act within our zones of agency, we transform our potential for joy into reality.

Tracking Joy: Strategic Growth Map

The Strategic Growth Map is a tool designed to help you reflect on your mental well-being and personal growth. It provides a visual representation of different zones, ranging from the Joyful Zone, where growth and determination thrive, to the Distressed Zone, where emotions like hopelessness and spiraling may be present. Identifying where you currently find yourself on this map enables you to better understand your emotional state and take intentional steps to create growth and joy.

Use the following reflection questions to assess your own growth:

- Which zone do you find yourself in today, and what factors have contributed to your current state?

- What specific actions can you take to move towards the Joyful Zone, even if it's just one step up?

- Reflect on a time when you were in the Joyful Zone. What practices or habits supported you then, and how can you integrate them now?

- How does being in the Neutral or Distressed Zone affect your overall well-being and relationships? What small shifts can you make to improve your experience

- What support or resources do you need to help you progress from your current zone to a more joyful one?

_____
_____
_____
_____
_____
_____
_____

Strategies for Practicing Joy

Tracking Joy: Strategic Growth Map

NOTES

Strategies for Practicing Joy

Strategies for Practicing Joy

Zones of Agency Reflection

The Zones of Agency are designed to help you examine the areas of your life where you have influence and control, and to reflect on how you can leverage that agency to create meaningful changes. Use the questions below to delve deeper into your experiences and explore how you can move towards greater liberation and fulfillment. Write the words that you remember experiencing in each square that reflects a past or current experience. Answer the reflection questions to further explore your zones of agency.

Which square do you resonate with most?

What compels people to experience liberation in their lives?

What causes people to stay stuck in the conflicted zone?

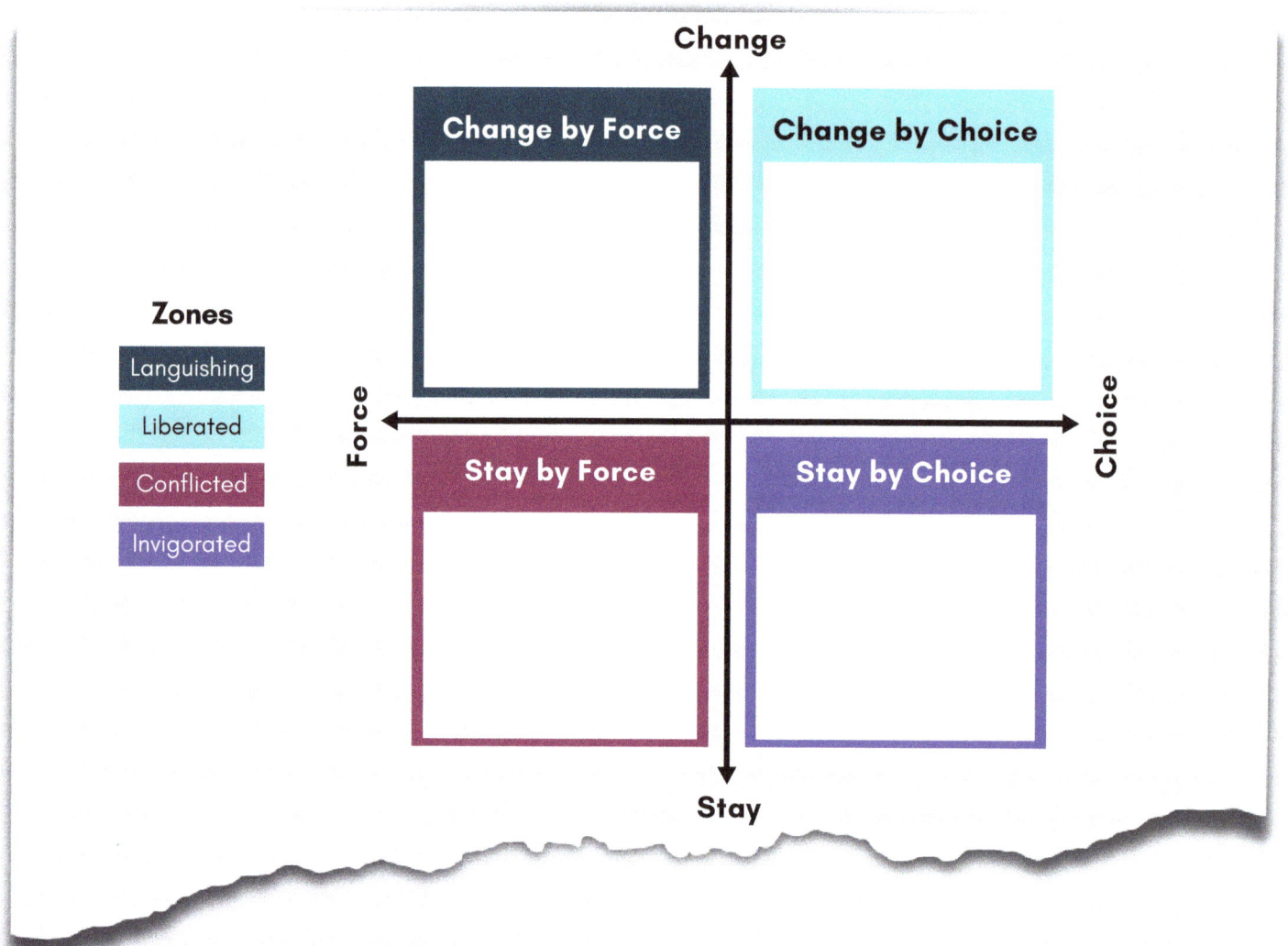

Zones of Agency Reflection
Sample Responses

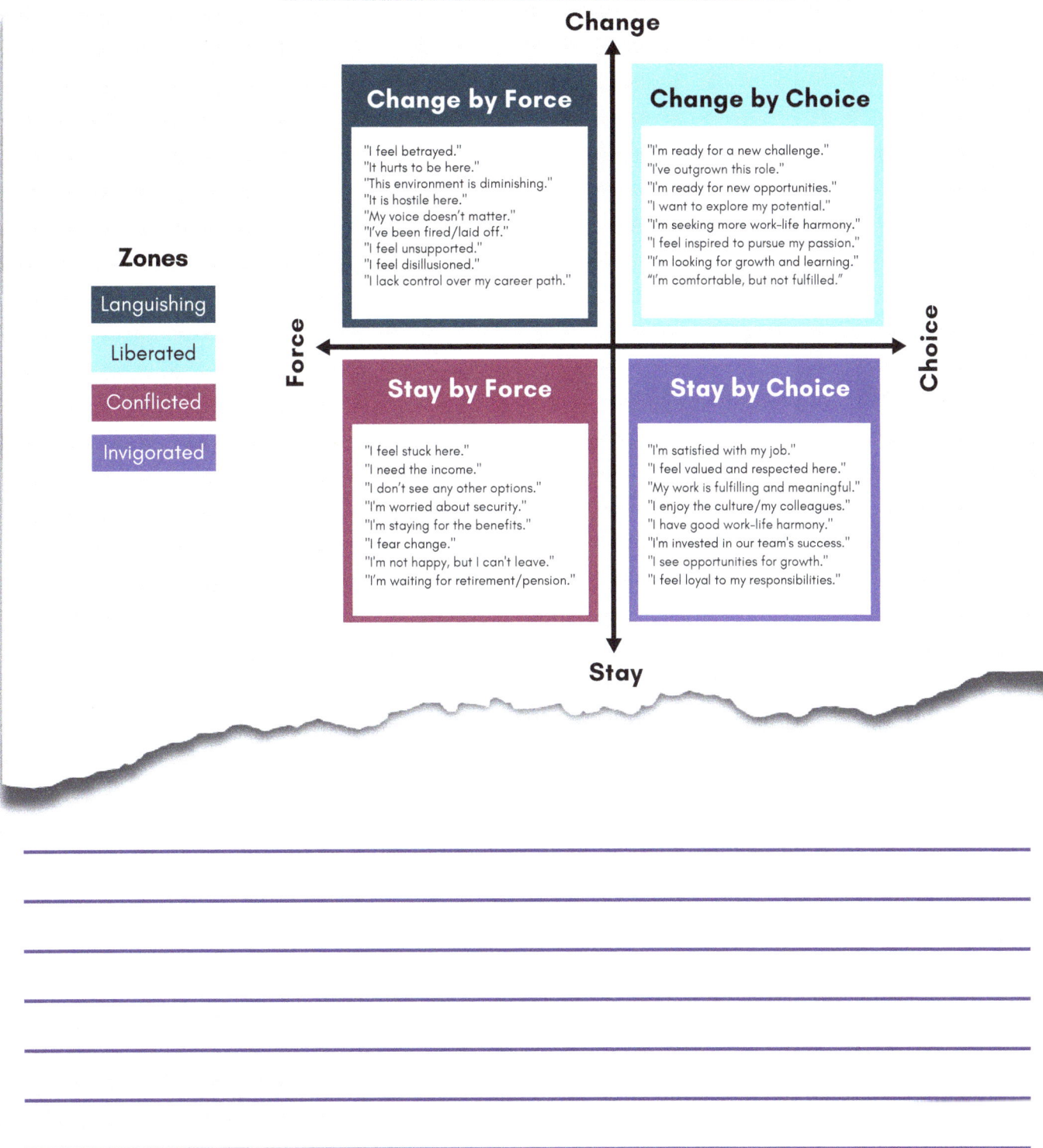

Strategies for Practicing Joy

EPIC Joy Strategies Worksheet

How will you commit to creating EPIC joy in your life? Use the chart below to map it out.

Establishing Well-Being	Positioning People	Integrating Joy	Creating Change

Notes

Notes

Reflection & Conclusion

Reflection & Conclusion

Reflecting on Your Journey

Looking back on your experience with this course, how has your understanding of joy evolved or deepened? Are there specific insights or moments that stand out to you as particularly impactful?

_____
_____
_____
_____
_____
_____
_____
_____

Personal Takeaways

What were the most significant personal takeaways from this course in relation to joy and its dimensions? How do you envision integrating these insights into your daily life?

_____
_____
_____
_____
_____
_____
_____
_____
_____

Reflection & Conclusion

Recognizing Growth

In what ways have you observed personal growth in your ability to embrace and cultivate joy? Can you identify instances where you applied the concepts learned in this course to overcome challenges?

_____
_____
_____
_____
_____
_____
_____

Barriers and Resilience

Have you encountered any of the barriers to joy discussed in this course since you started this journey? How did you respond differently, armed with the knowledge and strategies you've gained?

_____
_____
_____
_____
_____
_____
_____
_____
_____

Reflection & Conclusion

Embracing Joy

How does the concept of joy resonate with you? How might you begin to apply this concept to your life moving forward, and what changes might that bring?

_____
_____
_____
_____
_____
_____
_____

Creating Joyful Environments

Reflect on the impact of curating your communities of joy and nurturing connections that uplift you. How can you continue to create environments that encourage joy for yourself and others?

_____
_____
_____
_____
_____
_____
_____
_____
_____

Reflection & Conclusion

Joyful Practices and Integration

Which practices of joy discussed in the course resonate with you the most? How can you weave these practices into your daily routine and professional endeavors?

_____
_____
_____
_____
_____
_____
_____

Setting Intentions

As you move forward, what specific intentions can you set for prioritizing joy in your personal and professional life? How can you ensure that joy remains a central theme in your journey?

_____
_____
_____
_____
_____
_____
_____
_____

Reflection & Conclusion

Supporting Others

How might you share the knowledge you've gained with others in your personal and professional circles? How can you contribute to creating a more joyful community around you?

_____
_____
_____
_____
_____
_____
_____

Next Steps

Based on your reflections, what immediate actions will you take to continue your pursuit of joy and growth? What specific goals or projects would you like to initiate or prioritize?

_____
_____
_____
_____
_____
_____
_____
_____
_____
_____

Reflection & Conclusion

Continued Learning

How might you continue to explore and expand your understanding of joy and its dimensions beyond this course? What additional resources or practices are you interested in exploring?

Gratitude & Closure

Take a moment to express gratitude for the journey you've undertaken in this course. How do you feel about the progress you've made and the potential impact of cultivating joy in your life?

_____
_____
_____
_____
_____
_____
_____
_____
_____
_____
_____
_____
_____
_____
_____
_____
_____
_____
_____
_____
_____
_____

Notes

Notes

About the Author

Dr. Pamela A. Larde is a multifaceted scholar, certified coach, and award-winning author based in Atlanta, Georgia. With a Ph.D. in Leadership, she shares her wealth of knowledge as Associate Professor of Leadership at Anderson University, but her passion for empowering others extends beyond academia as Founder and President of the Academy of Creative Coaching and Director of Education at the Institute of Coaching.

An accomplished writer, with glowing reviews from Writer's Digest and Publisher's Weekly, Dr. Pamela's notable publications include, Amazon Bestseller, *Joyfully Single* (2023), the award-winning and best-selling *Letters to the Brokenhearted* (2013), and the *Color Your Life* book series (2015), which she co-authored with her cousin, Pernethia Arrington. Additionally, Dr. Pamela channels her first love for communication into her podcast, *The Joy Whisperer*, which is her playground for profound conversations around the practice and science of joy.

Raised in a tight-knit family, Dr. Pamela is a proud mother of two children, Daniel and Jóia, and their Shih-Poo, Prince. Her love for travel and writing in quaint restaurants complements her commitment to creating joy wherever possible, especially when writing.

Dr. Pamela developed *The Practice of Joy* course to help participants incorporate joy into their personal and professional lives. She employs her unique experiences in leadership, as well as her academic and professional coach training, to support people from all walks of life grappling with the struggle to find joy.

Follow Dr. Pamela's journey and join her community of joy through her website, www.DrPamelaLarde.com, and her social media platforms under the handle @joyresearcher. Through her body of work, Dr. Pamela continues to spark a joyous revolution, demonstrating to the world that joy can indeed be a way of life.

www.ingramcontent.com/pod-product-compliance
Lightning Source LLC
Chambersburg PA
CBHW061420090426
42744CB00020B/2079